Changing Places

Carl Tomlinson

for my family

Fair Acre Press

First published in Great Britain on 31st July 2021 by Fair Acre Press
www.fairacrepress.co.uk

ISBN 978-1-911048-51-0
Typeset and Cover Design by Nadia Kingsley
Cover image © Carl Tomlinson 2021

Acknowledgements

I am grateful to the following readers, listeners and editors who have
offered encouragement and insight:

Claire Cox, Samantha Day, Clare Hart, Julia Iball, Jenny Lewis, Hannah Lowe,
Hamish MacCall, Sarah MacCall, Christina Morton, Helena Nelson,
Liz Nicholson, Jacob Polley, Jean Sprackland, and the members of Oxford
Stanza 2 and The Next Step. The Catweazle Club in Oxford and Scriptstuff in
Banbury have been fertile proving grounds – thank you to Matt Sage and Mike
Took for creating these spaces.

Special thanks to Sarah J Bryson and Alan Buckley who helped me to get my
writing going again, and to Helen Mort who helped me to get it to here.

Dupuytren's: your hand in mine was first published on gooddadhood.com in
2017.

Reintroduction was first published in the 2017 Ver Prize Anthology, and
Cherwell valley nightscape was first published in The Scriptstuff Lockdown
Anthology in 2020.

Contents

The lie of the land 5

Farm

Baling 7

Milk Marketing 8

Toy 9

Coming to grief 10

They moved our sky 12

Inventory 13

Dupuytren's: your hand in mine 14

Fold

Picking sides 16

Present 17

New forest 18

Hair loss 20

Before your father's funeral 21

To David on your 50th birthday 22

Stayers 23

Fields

Reintroduction 26

Sunshine in Oxford in early October 27

Off road 28

Cherwell valley nightscape 29

Slide 30

Petrichor 31

August 32

Cocksure 33

Harvest 34

..on the sign it said "No Trespassing"
But on the other side it didn't say nothing.
That side was made for you and me

Woody Guthrie - *This land is your land*

The lie of the land

The lie of the land
says she is ours to command
will yield to the strongest hand

that we may mark it as home
fence it off as our own
keep out the unwelcome unknown.

The slugs and the rats and the weeds
know nothing of title deeds,
don't care about heritage seeds.

The pigeons, the pheasants and rooks
haven't read the Domesday book.
They just shit on my dirty looks.

The lie of the land
says a man *is* an island,
that we are where we stand,
that it's ours and not yours
and the world isn't there any more
when we slide the bolt on the door,

that we're safer alone,
that we need clearer zones
and that we can tame it with drones.

This is the lie of the land,
that wall and fence and gate
make an independent state.

Farm

Baling

I'd just got my A-levels out of the way
and was spending a week with my Aunt
in the house her grandfather'd built
in the garden behind the farm,
in a place that had seemed like forever, aged eight.
She said "Derek Fitton wants a hand with his hay."
As kids we had loved helping Grandad,
chasing the baler round Tandle Hill's haunch
riding the trailer back to the barn
echoing Tarzan calls under the bridge.
We lived with the itching and the seeds in our hair
because that was the way we were made.
It was ten years since the pain of the sale
and I wanted to feel like a farmer again.
Derek was glad of my help that day.
It was fun enough, in a blokeish way.
He gave me a fiver. Later, I drank it away.
The twine cut my fingers, my back complained
the welts sprang up on my arms again.
You wouldn't know, I guess you've never baled
but it's a different kind of ache when it's not your hay.

Milk Marketing

The lane's a potholed midden. The David Brown bucks
over each ridge and rut. My teeth find every bump.

We heave full churns on the milkstand down at the Cow,
where they hunch like six squashed sentries. We lift six empties
and get them on the –
  It had a name which I've forgotten.
And it hung behind the tractor. I clung on.

Once you went round daily with the horse,
pouring milk from door to door and at Christmas,
as my Dad reminds me every Christmas,
a half was poured for you at every pub you served.
You'd take each one and hand the reins to him.

A year from now, before the farm is sold,
an antiseptic, always cold, stainless steel container
beside the milking parlour will gather two days' yield
for when the tanker churns the lane
and sucks in sterilised efficiency
the milk you never touch and scarcely see.

Toy

Beasts and fields and milk
meant muck and sweat and aches
before baths, then tea and bed.

Grading eggs was child's play
the chance to operate that bathroom-blue
part-bagatelle, part-bowling-alley
where work was done by gravity
in a mood you might call levity.

Warm in the palm, the morning's eggs
were fed along a gentle slope
to roll down chutes which matched their size.
Outgrades and breakages didn't go to waste.
They were fried for breakfasts, baked in cakes.

It turns out that my toy was worth
more than most men made in a week.
It must have saved a lot of work.

Coming to grief

We were most of the way to Middleton
when I discovered that grief
doesn't always dress in death.
One of my parents said
that Three Gates Farm –
where six generations had tilled
the last of Lancashire's silty soil –
was being sold that week.

In the winter of sixty-three
my Grandad made the front page
phoning for a snowplough
because the lane was six foot deep.
Now we were in 'th'Observer' again
in the back of the classifieds
along with all the other lots
due 'Under the Marshall hammer.'

Reading the paper emptied my eyes.
I realised whatever childish plans I'd made
for those fifty acres of gentle land
nudged between mill towns and millstone grit
were to be knocked down
(for twenty-six grand in the end)
in Ye Olde Boar's Head
by an auctioneer I never met.

And by my father's teenage need to leave that land
and make his life his own.
And by my uncle's trying to stay
where I was sure we all belonged.
And by Grandad's explaining

that even the hencotes would go.
So the scheme to keep one to use as a den,
that went south as well.

The parlour's long since seen a cow,
there's nothing like a farm there now
but the breath of beasts on a winter day
and the sweetness of cowshit and hay
surprise that grief back into me.

They moved our sky

when they banked up the earth
to sling the motorway over the fields.
There's a kink in Hough Lane
where the bridge dragged it yards to the north.
Everyone reckoned it did for the drainage.
The puddles and slutch suggest they were right.

Dad says folk always knew which was Tomlinson land.
Our grass was greenest
because Joseph would put his muck back
while others sold theirs for ready cash.
This kept the earth rich so roots went deeper.
And a little compensation came,
for what the tarmac took away.

Those riches now are gathered here
by will and trust and deed
in the fields that I tread every day
to check the sheep,
or to see what's new
among the trees which frame the view
I sometimes think I own.

Inventory

Accounts and correspondence,
attached with failing staples,
complete the detail of a sale
of *Live and Dead Farming Stock.*

Dead just means inanimate,
not deceased.

Then, in the *Particulars,* I find the line
that honours my line, and all they left here
'The land will be seen to be
in a high state of fertility.'

Dupuytren's: your hand in mine

For Joseph Tomlinson 1908-1986

The doctor tells me that this gristle in my palm
is Dupuytren's,
a thickening of soft tissue
which can leave the finger bent.

I'm back with Grandad on Tandle Hill.
Holding his hand, I look down on the farm,
see him swing that four-stone weight,
the one he used for spuds,
with only his little finger!

His hands – great mud-scored tubers –
wrestled pens to form his name
and cuffed me just the once
for scaring fish down at the cut
then lay milk-cold and udder-pink
across his empty chest.

Years later I guess that the super-strong finger
was stiff with Dupuytren's.
Today I feel that hand in mine
and know we're bound
not by this name I carry
not by that strength I thought I saw
but by shared frailty.

Fold

Picking sides

FA Cup Final. 1 May 1976. Southampton 1 – 0 Manchester United

Bobby Stokes made me a Red
one Spring day at Wembley.
He broke my heart in a moment
scuffing that shot past Stepney.

Although I wasn't football mad
you still had to pick a side
and a playground full of Saints fans
said Man United were mine.

Four years after moving South
my accent was still abused.
Flattened vowels lurked in my mouth
and echoed round the school.

All that week I learned their names
eager to share the glory,
but sometimes, as the pundits say,
the Cup's a fairy story.

Nil-nil at eighty-three minutes,
the telly rings with cheers.
Stokes shoots. He scores. Saints win it.
This was what I'd feared.

Bobby Stokes made me blush deep red
at hymn-time in assembly,
For all the saints, the teacher said.
Every face was turned on me.

Present

Birthdays and Christmas meant Lego,
your uncle and me sprawled on the floor
making the kits, then setting bricks free
to capture space in canting walls.

Between the bursts of energy
which shaped our glimpsed creations,
in the frustration of scale,
the being bound by doors and wheels
then seeing halfway up, or in,
the step we'd missed in the urge to begin,
bits of us, scraped no doubt from ear or nose,
were smeared into these piles of plastic.

This morning, as you two root among them
proffering the perfect parts
for me to make a Scoop or Muck or Dizzy,
something of those boys lies on this floor
lodged in the teeth marks of hurried demolition,
smudging the material of shared imagination.

New forest

Leaving the motorway at Cadnam
we cross the cattle grid.
You are entering the New Forest.
'Where are all the trees?' you say
as we drive through heathland
gorsed to yellow beneath a canopy of sky.
All's a lot to ask. All's nine hundred years
of growth, decay and management.

An arrow cut from one punctured Rufus' lung,
hundreds more were sailed and sunk.
Some still sludge the Solent,
their salvaged neighbours pickle in a flagship's hulk.
This podsol's metres deep with them,
they're the black in the Blackwater's water.

Returning bombers opened craters
where no root can hold
and the acrid ash of '76
when acre after acre burnt for weeks
is scattered past imagination's reach.
Ponies nibble saplings,
pannage fattened pigs devour
beeches you will never see.

The forest's only New because it wasn't here
before the Normans brought the word to English ears.
It's bigger now, this playground
of natives and invaders
where our energetic gang once traced racetracks.
We canoodled in its thickets
we came to think of it as home.
That boy's back yard, which once was Ytten,
then a King's preserve, is now a National Park.

But still its seeds are flown and blown
beyond boundaries drawn in any legend.
They land in gardens, they muscle into hedges,

and one, I like to dream
became this notebook that I leaf
trying to show you where to see the trees.

Hair loss

Mum dragged us uphill to the barber where,
sat on a plank, we were steel-combed and fringed.
Our annual school photos show bowl-rimmed grins.
"You've got a calf-lick, you can't have long hair."
                    My brother died with his tight light curls
                    reduced to a wisp here and there.

In interview week she gave me a trim
though shaggier boys would also get in.
The earring which for years was forbidden
now shone in my newly visible lobe.
Dad admired the haircut, "Much smarter short."
I showed off the stud, to show him I'd dared.
"You were told not to have that." No more.
                    In death her hair was a half-inch
                    of velvet, the wig went in the bin.

Late one evening they hacked at my curls
for charity in the college bar,
a quid a snip for research for a cure.

Before your father's funeral
for Hamish

I got here early so I popped to Reeves.
The coffee's better than it used to be.
The lardy cake still has a taste of home
though it was never quite as good as Mum's.
I've been looking for us in places we went
when we were hellbent on becoming men
and found that even the ones that remain
have moved on a bit since we went away.

They sell vibrators in the George Mall now
in an Ann Summers packed with perky toys
absurdly at odds with the passing tweeds
who still come to town for market-day treats.
It's round the corner from the chemist's shop
where I first cringed a packet of condoms.
After I'd whispered how many, what sort,
she passed them over the counter, bored.

Salisbury back then wore lace-ups and pearls
and sex was something it kept tightly furled.
On hot afternoons we'd skip triple games
sprawled on the grass in The Close in the arms
of maybe the Mums of these friendly staff
who this morning arrange fluffy handcuffs
and recommend lube with smiling advice.
Our mothers would have told us, 'Avert your eyes.'

The coffee's cold. I just wanted to tell you
that somehow this city has grown up too.

To David on your 50th birthday

'Santa Claus is coming to town'

Springsteen on the radio gurning that Christmas tune,
Doris – who'd babysat and watched Pot Black with us –
waiting with me in another room
because I didn't have
whatever it took
to sit there and watch you die.

In between

A day or two later
I lifted the lace they'd put over your face,
unprepared for the shock of that look,
or the lock of what was left of your hair.

23rd December 1985

You know death was no stranger at school,
most years in a morning assembly
we'd learn how some biker had come off the roll
but those pews of your classmates' faces
in St Mary's that Monday
said cancer doesn't come for sixteen-year-olds.

A windy Saturday, a month or two later

For a skinny kid who'd been so ill
you made a lot of ash.
As you danced across the churchyard,
wilder than you had ever dared.

8th February 2019

The label on the flowers
on your coffin read
"To a wonderful son
and brother." Dad chose the words.
I hedged the adjective, nodding a numb "OK."
This morning the air is chill in my lungs
as I check up on things in the field
and you've got me wondering now.
About the last breath that you drew
the one I never knew. I test it in this silence,
the one that left you still and
still leaves me,
leaves me the only brother.

Stayers

Some of the boys I started school with
now lay carpets in my father's house.
Girls who shared games of kiss chase
are carers, or clean for his neighbours.
They're the ones with countless cousins
whose grandmas picked them up from school.
Their surnames fill the graveyard
and punctuate the war memorial.

Every village has its stayers, its plasterers,
farmers and footie players.
Round here they drink in the Red
early doors. Same pint, same seat,
some are in their seventies, some still need ID.

The headstones at St John's say that
we were stayers once, my Dad's lot anyway.
On trips back to the farm somebody
would always say "That's Joe's grandson."
"It's bloody not," growled Dad, "that's *my* lad."

It's not listlessness, or lack of life chances
that keeps them here, and there.
They aren't kept anyway
they stay.
                    Sure, you can say the eleven-plus,
the need to catch the early bus
was my ticket to the better grades
to a life lived at another's pace
but I don't remember thinking
I could settle in that place,
or get what it takes
if I didn't get away.

Fields

Reintroduction

When I was a boy
and the world was much bigger
and nature walks counted as lessons,
while willow was still in the dictionary,
my eyes could fathom the sky.

When I was a student
and Stokenchurch white
and Didcot still clouded the view,
Spanish and Swedish raptors arrived,
coasting tarmac, claiming its kill.

These days I'm a Dad,
and Stokenchurch green.
At Didcot the towers are dry.
Ungrounded my eyes fight my neck for perspective
as the raptors reshape the sky.

These birds encompass
too much of the view,
for something flying so high.
The kites are reintroducing
the man to the boy and his sky.

Sunshine in Oxford in early October

chisels the stone, bleaches the High,
gives this air a bite

was low enough to show off
the promise of curves and blind us to their risk

casts a 30 year shadow
behind me, safe out of reach

made us look stunning in subfusc

surrenders too early to dusk

Off road

for CWD

'never yawn or say a commonplace thing'
Jack Kerouac On The Road

Hi mate, guess what,
I gave my Kerouac posters
(which I'd used to put my heart
into an office I don't need)
to a housemate of our son's
who'd come up to read the Beats.
She still saw On The Road as
something like a dream.

Do you remember, Skips, when
we thought we were Sal and Dean?
All nighters, emptying ourselves
and countless crates of beer.
Now we walk the footpaths
and talk proudly of our lads
safe in the kind of silence
those wild boys used to fear.

Cherwell valley nightscape

14 April 2020

No contrails blur the stars.
The Oxford road is free of cars.

All I hear is train wheels ringing distant rails.
Somewhere near a hunting owl screeches for a mate.

The Milky Way's a champagne spume
unchallenged by an absent moon.

I borrow a breath of this shining air.
The vastness swallows what I offer in return.

Slide

for BS

He's back. Forty years after his arse
scraped that mark in the side of the bank,
he's brought her to where the bedrock
still shines, where he and his mates
tore down the slope on cardboard boxes
they'd pinched from Fairbrace's mill.

"We were motorbikes, tanks, racing cars, planes."

Bit by bit they ripped out the grass,
then Lancashire's leftover rain swept the soil
into the Calder's carpet-dye water.
Oak trees have rooted around his line in the land.
He turns. She smiles.

They swing out of town on a ring-road
scarred on the face of the place where he grew.

Petrichor

for JI

'Philosophy will clip an Angel's wings
Conquer all mysteries by rule and line
Empty the haunted air'
John Keats *Lamia*

It's worth a little rain sometimes
to feel the earth is alive
to smell beneath a darkened sky
the sweetness that flies from the fields

After the hiss of the cloudburst
at the kiss of a few fresh drops
the scent of a thousand flowers drifts
from the heat of sunbaked soil.

I like the way the term,
which I only recently heard,
refuses to unweave this molecule
allows us to believe a little more than what is true

This magic, named for the blood of the gods,
promises growth as it fumes.
It's worth a little rain sometimes
to scent the world in bloom.

August

All along the bridleway
some kind of rain
is trying to shake off the wind.
The land feels thinned.

Cocksure

A minute before a midwinter dawn
he opens his beak to call up the sun.
Hearing my footfall he gives me the eye
then casts me aside. He's dared me to write
what he apprehends.
               I water the hens,
head back in the house for paper and pen.
He's busy filling his gizzard with grit.
I'm scratting round for morsels of wit.
He's out shrieking the sky into light.
I sit cursing and creasing pages of white.

Harvest

"Oh bugger!" The words thud.
I've just put the fork through a spud.

I'm showing our son and daughter
something I learnt from my father
which my Grandad had taught him before.

"You start a bit off, away from the green,
keep the fork away from the tubers,
you want to lift 'em, not pierce 'em,
and they'll not store if you fork 'em,
they'll be no good if you fork 'em'."

Again the fork sinks, again the soil shifts
and this time a big'un gets stuck on a tine.
"Oh bugger!" I thud before I'm stood up
and quick as an echo the lad pipes up
with "That's what our Grandad said
when he put his fork through a spud."

About the Author

Carl was born in Lancashire – where his father's family had farmed for 150 years – and moved to Wiltshire as a child. He has clear and fond memories of working with his grandfather – making hay, milking cows and lifting potatoes. He attended Bishop Wordsworth's School in Salisbury before reading Spanish and French at St Catherine's College, Oxford. By his 21st birthday he had buried half his immediate family.

After qualifying as a Chartered Accountant, Carl spent most of his career working with his father as a director of a metal-finishing business. He studied for an MA in Coaching and Mentoring at Oxford Brookes University. He is now a coach and part-time finance director.

Carl and his wife Kate live with their dog on a smallholding in Oxfordshire. They have two adult children.

Despite writing a lot as a teenager he stopped after leaving school, only starting again in earnest after chance encounters with the Oxfordshire writers Sarah J Bryson and Alan Buckley. He regularly reads at open-mic events and at the Catweazle Club in Oxford. He has been published in magazines, anthologies and online. His poem *Market Forces* won Oxford City Council's competition to celebrate the Covered Market and will shortly form part of an audio installation there.

Milton Keynes UK
Ingram Content Group UK Ltd.
UKHW021653270324
440125UK00007BA/162